This Candlewick book
belongs to:

_____

_____

_____

STOMP AND CHOMP: MY FIRST BOOK OF DINOSAURS

SIMON MOLE

ILLUSTRATED BY MATT HUNT

CANDLEWICK PRESS

CONTENTS

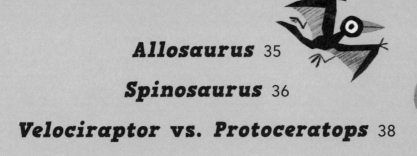

ABOUT THIS BOOK

In these pages, you'll find dinosaurs of every shape and size—from long-necked leaf munchers as big as buses to little feathery fighters with beaks, and a full gamut in between.

Some of them seem so incredible, so unlikely, so wonderfully weird, that it's easy to forget one of the most amazing things about them: that they actually existed—stomping (or scuttling) their way around the very same planet we live on today! In fact, dinosaurs lived ALL OVER the globe: in deserts, rain forests, swamps, even on snow and ice. We think they ruled the earth for around 180 million years, and if you compare that to the few million years we humans have been around, you'll start to get a sense of just how long that is.

Some hunted at top speed, munching huge mouthfuls of meat in one go. Some plodded about slowly, nibbling leaves. Some had claws as long as swords and peacock-style feathery tails. At least that's what we think. But it's exciting to remember that there are lots of things about dinosaurs that even experts don't know for certain. It's important to keep curious about them, to keep asking *What if . . . ?* This question might just lead us to our next big dinosaur discovery.

Take a look at the dinosaurs on the right. Maybe you can spot some you already know. Are there any you'd like to know more about?

There are? Well, you're in the right place!

MEET THE DINOSAURS

TRICERATOPS
(try-SAIR-uh-tops)

Look out—it's *Triceratops*! Run! Run!

The three-horned warrior! Run! Run!

The ten-ton champion! Running! Running!

The huge-headed hero . . . is running away!

TYRANNOSAURUS REX
(tih-RAN-uh-SAWR-us reks)

From its terrible teeth to the tip of its tail,

T. rex is longer than five lions laid in a line,

with a footprint 2½ times bigger than

the book in your hand.

T. rex is **HUGE**.

Every day it needs to eat more than

200 pounds (100 kilograms) of dinosaur meat.

That's 500 burgers a day!

T. rex is HUNGRY.

So it HUNTS and it HUNTS and it HUNTS . . .

ARGENTINOSAURUS
(ahr-jen-TEEN-uh-SAWR-us)

A body as big as a double-decker bus
with legs as tall as tree trunks beneath
and a noodly neck as long as a crane . . .
Just imagine how much it could eat!

BARYONYX
(BAIR-ee-ON-iks)

Swift sprinter

Tail flicker

River watcher

Quick dasher

Fish grabber

Flesh ripper

Best hunter

Gets dinner!

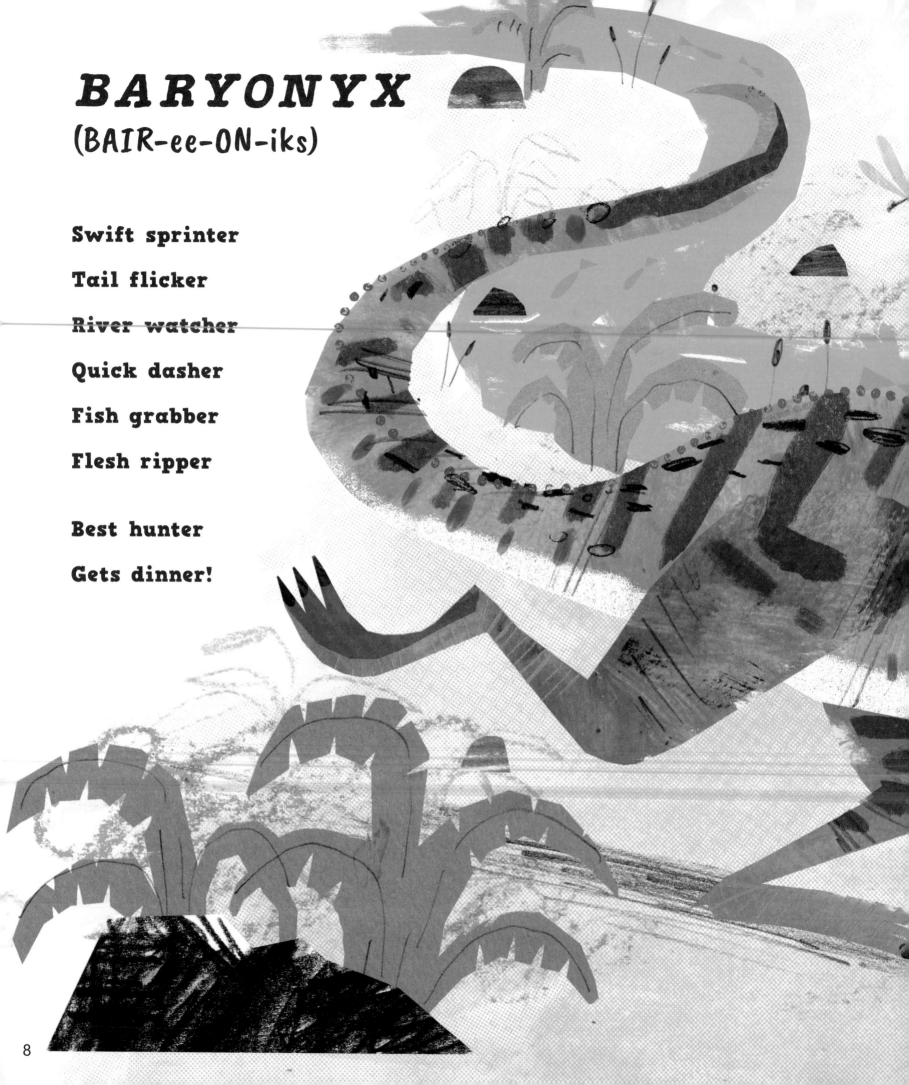

COELOPHYSIS

(SEE-lo-FIE-sis)

You're a slowpoke and I'm so **faaaaast**.

If we had a race, you would come in **laaaaast**.

Silly swamp-lizard, just **waddling around**.
You still keep **all four legs** on the **ground**.

With your legs out to the side
and your tummy in the **swamp**,
you will never catch me, I can never be—**CHOMP!**

GIGANOTOSAURUS
(JIG-uh-NOT-uh-SAWR-us)

A *Giganotosaurus*'s head is the size of a human.

Just its head, bigger than the whole of your body!

Just its TONGUE, bigger than the whole of your body!

A huge, hot, slobbery slab of wibbly muscle,

long enough for you to lie down on

with your arms stretched out over your head.

A tongue. Big enough. To be your bed.

BRACHIOSAURUS
(BRAK-ee-uh-SAWR-us)

One *Brachiosaurus* weighs the same as 30 cars.

Or 80 cows. Or 100 grand pianos.

Which is the same as 350 reindeer.

Or 10,000 cats.

TEN. THOUSAND. CATS.

Imagine how many leaves

you would need to eat

to weigh as much as that!

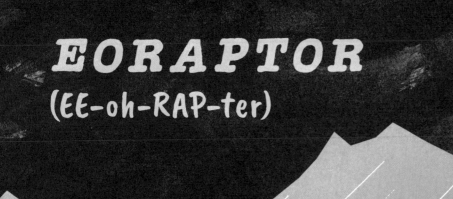

EORAPTOR
(EE-oh-RAP-ter)

I was one of the first!

Small as a dog, tiny and tough,

in a world of dry deserts, volcanoes, and floods—

on the run from fierce creatures much bigger than me.

I'm a survivor . . . and I need to be!

THERIZINOSAURUS: A RECIPE

(THAIR-uh-ZEEN-uh-SAWR-us)

Carefully remove one evil sea serpent

from a fairy tale or myth,

then whack it on the body

of an oversize potbellied ostrich.

Grab a fancy feathery peacock tail

and heat it in the shape-shifter

until it quadruples in size.

Add it to the mix. Leave to settle.

Now here's the final touch!

Six swords, roughly the length of your arm.

Sprinkle three on each side,

and stand well back.

A Cretaceous specialty

best served with caution.

EDMONTOSAURUS
(ed-MON-tuh-SAWR-us)

I'm a super snacker—I munch on the move.

Breakfast, dinner, lunch on the move.

Can't stop for long, 'cause if I do,

this super snacker might become a snack too!

HALSZKARAPTOR
(HAHL-shkuh-RAP-ter)

So quick! *Zip! Zip!*

Tail flick! *Zip! Zip!*

A *Halszkaraptor* darts out of the ferns.

So quick! *Zip! Zip!*

Tail flick! *Sniff! Sniff!*

Prowling the shoreline, watching the water,

the shimmering shadows beneath.

Are you hungry enough to come hunting

where others see YOU as something to eat?

STEGOSAURUS
(STEG-uh-SAWR-us)

A line of warning signs along its back.

A line of giant kite-shaped armored plates.

Some even say they flushed with blood

to change color

and send their message out:

LEAVE ME ALONE!

NOT IN THE MOOD!

DON'T TRY ME!

HAVE YOU SEEN THE SIZE OF THE SPIKES ON MY TAIL?

MORE THAN ENOUGH

If you eat the big leaves from the top of the tree

and I feast on the ferns near the ground,

there's more than enough, there's more than enough,

there's MORE than enough to go round!

GIRAFFATITAN
(juh-RAF-uh-TIE-tun)

CAMAROSAURUS
(KAM-uh-ruh-SAWR-us)

EUROPASAURUS
(yuh-RO-puh-SAWR-us)

If you tear the tough twigs from the trunk with your teeth,

I'll munch all the soft, sweet leaves to be found.

There's more than enough, there's more than enough,

there's MORE than enough to go round!

CEDAROSAURUS
(SEE-duh-ro-SAWR-us)

Cedarosaurus doesn't chew. Not once. Ever.

It gulps its leaves and twigs down whole,

and then it swallows stones—

small rounded rocks

that roll around in its tummy,

bashing and grinding up leaves,

mashing and pounding down leaves—

thousands of leaves

slowly rotting inside its belly,

like a massive moving compost bin.

Just imagine the smell when you

breathe it in!

DINOSAUR DROPPINGS

Some dinosaur dung (that's poop to me and you)

is almost twice as big as a basketball.

Just one poop like that could crush

a toilet flat. *Whump. Splat. Smash.*

Not all dinosaur dung

is enormous: some

dinos drop plops

as small as

a tiny

pea.

PACHYCEPHALOSAURUS

(pak-ih-SEF-uh-luh-SAWR-us)

Biff-a-bash. Biff-a-bash.
Bang-a-lang-a-bop.

My head is like a helmet or a very heavy rock,

so we biff-a-bash our heads until we *both* know who is boss.

Biff-a-bash. Biff-a-bash.
Bang-a-lang-a-bop!

ALLOSAURUS
(AL-uh-SAWR-us)

Hack, hack, hatchet-head.

Jerk right back, jaws wide open.

Hack, hack, stab and rip.

Rip and chew. Jaws wide

Open. Jaws clamp shut. That's that.

Hatchet-head. Hack, hack.

SPINOSAURUS
(SPY-nuh-SAWR-us)

They say *T. rex* is the biggest carnivore, but I am!

They say dinosaurs can't swim, but I can!

A snout like a supersize crocodile mouth,

so I'm getting jealous looks from any crocodiles around.

I know it sounds wild, but I tell you it's true:

even the fish on my dish is bigger than you!

They say dinosaurs can't swim, but I can!

They say *T. rex* is the biggest carnivore, but I am!

VELOCIRAPTOR vs.

(vuh-LOSS-uh-RAP-ter)

Deadly toe claw

Dagger teeth

        Fancy frill neck

        Snappy beak

Fast and feathered

Speedy thief

        Slow and scaly

        Nibbling leaves

Leg grabbers

        Arm biters

Neck stabbers

        Desert fighters!

PROTOCERATOPS

PROTOCERATOPS
(PRO-to-SAIR-uh-tops)

VELOCIRAPTOR

DINOSAUR FAMILIES

BABY *DIPLODOCUS*
(dih-PLOD-uh-kus)

One hundred baby diplodocuses

hatch beneath the forest floor

and clamber free from buried eggs.

They push their tiny wet heads toward fresh air.

POP! One sprouts out from the soil.

POP! POP! Two more.

The clearing quickly crowds

with new life seeking sunlight:

a dinosaur garden in full bloom.

PLANET ON LEGS

Now that I'm full-grown,

I'm so very, very big

that small animals live

their whole lives on my back!

Every snack, every sleep,

their whole lives on my back.

Every scratch, every squeak,

their whole lives on my back.

A planet on legs, just plodding along—

plodding, a-plodding along.

DIPLODOCUS

THE HERD

A herd means nuzzling necks.

Thousands of tails that talk

with flicks and swishes and thwacks.

A herd means sticking together no matter what.

Leaving that last luscious leaf

for another mouth to munch.

A herd means feeling at home wherever you are.

A soft tingly glow in your tummy.

Knowing you belong.

PARASAUROLOPHUS ECHOES (PAIR-uh-saw-RAWL-uh-fus)

When a *Parasaurolophus* blows air

through the tubes and passageways in its crest,

when its breath whooshes up the little tunnels inside,

it lets out a long . . . low . . . bellowing . . . cry.

Scientifically shown to be a similar sound

to a cow playing a trumpet in a cave.

Or a goose troupe tooting kazoos.

Or one very grizzly goat

with a didgeridoo.

And, OK, that got a little silly, but

imagine hundreds and hundreds in a herd:

each calling to another, back and forth.

A constant chorus. Deep. Majestic.

Echoing for miles and miles.

Echoing through the forest.

Echoing up past the treetops

and out into the sky.

TOUGH! TOUGH! TOUGH!

Thick-skinned, thorny tanks. Thunder tails—*thump, thud!*

Oversize ogres.

Utterly unbreakable.

Gently grazing greenery. *Grunt. Grunt. Grunt.*

Huge hulking, hard-headed herbivores.

TOUGH!

ANKYLOSAURUS
(ANG-kuh-lo-SAWR-us)

EUOPLOCEPHALUS
(YOO-oh-plo-SEF-uh-lus)

SAUROPELTA
(sawr-oh-PEL-tuh)

SUPER SWIMMERS

(Not really dinosaurs, still really awesome)

Ichthyosaurus
(ik-thee-uh-SAWR-us)

A slick, speedy shadow in dark **water**

Darting through the deep like a dolphin

Huge eyes to hunt fish in the gloom

Rhomaleosaurus
(ro-muh-LEE-uh-SAWR-us)

Super-strong swimmers

We fly through the **water**

Flapping all four flippers at once

Kronosaurus (KRON-oh-SAWR-us)

Two times as long as a great white shark

Bone-crunching teeth in giant jaws

One of the biggest reptile to ever swim in **water**

PTEROSAURS

(Not really dinosaurs, still really awesome)

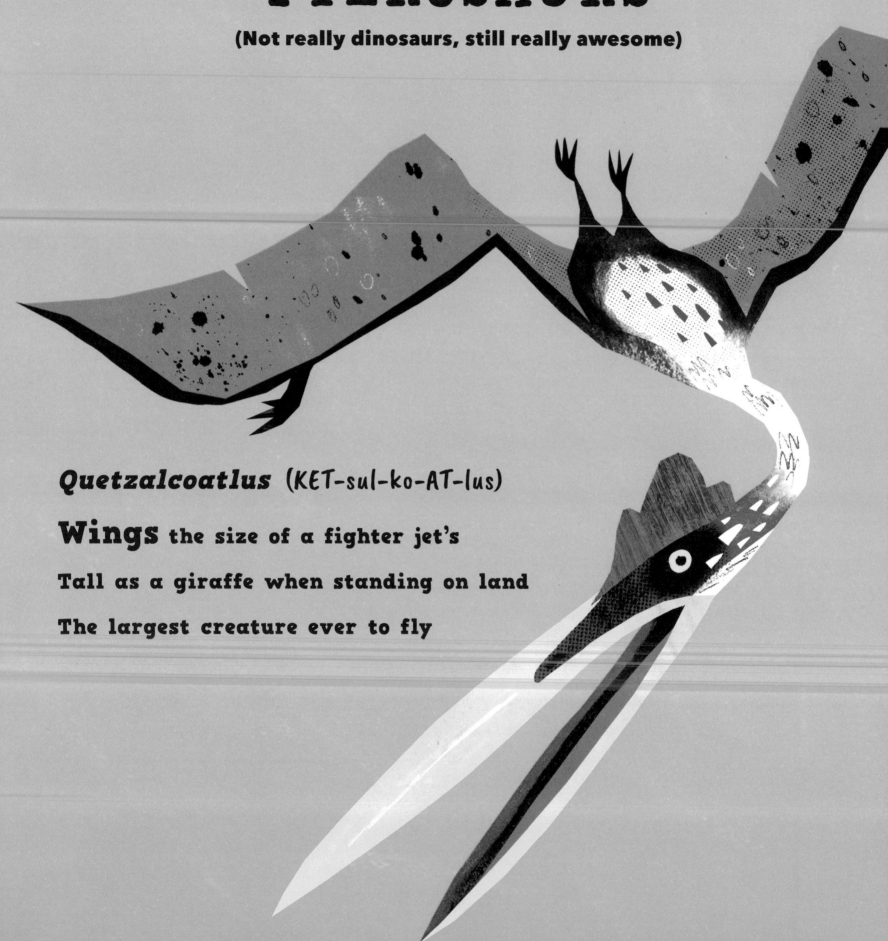

Quetzalcoatlus (KET-sul-ko-AT-lus)

Wings the size of a fighter jet's

Tall as a giraffe when standing on land

The largest creature ever to fly

Pteranodon (tuh-RAN-uh-don)

Wings to swoop down

Long beak without teeth

Scooping up fish from the sea

Rhamphorhynchus
(ram-fuh-RINK-us)

Wings with real power

A tail like a kite, tipped with a diamond

For steering a path through the skies

HERRERASAURUS
(huh-RAIR-uh-SAWR-us)

Do I look familiar? Like somebody famous

but a little bit . . . littler?

You see, there were lots of us *Herrerasauruses*,

but the ones with longer legs were quicker runners.

The ones with bigger heads were better hunters.

The better hunters had a better chance to survive:

to stay alive longer and have babies,

with bigger heads and longer legs,

just like Mommy.

Tiny changes. Taking ages. Bit by bit.

We grew bigger. Stronger. Faster.

Bit by bit. For millions of years . . .

Until we looked so different,

we were a whole new dinosaur.

Without me, there would be no *T. rex*!

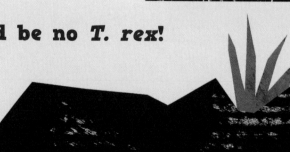

A VOLCANO ERUPTS

There is **lava** four times hotter than fire
underneath the earth's crust.
We call it **magma** until it erupts.

When things move around down there,
it gets pushed up through the surface
like a red-hot river of earth blood.

So much smoke, so much dust!
Lava runs faster than a dinosaur does!
Flattening forests and swallowing up EVERYTHING in its path . . .

59

THE ASTEROID

A giant flaming space rock, seven miles wide,

smashes into Earth at 40 times the speed a bullet flies!

Earth shudders, shakes. Earth judders, quakes.

Earth ripples—solid ground gone bendy,

hurls huge dinos off their feet and up into the sky!

A storm of flaming rocks rains down:

a cloud of thick space dust and ash

that hovers over Earth for years,

so all beneath is dark.

And still, some dinosaurs survive . . .

THE END.
OR IS IT?

CHICKEN?!
(CHIK-un)

"I survived! When is it my page?"

You're just a chicken.

You don't roar; you cluck and coo.

This is not the book for you. Shoo!

"Wait! What if I told you that my great-great-great-great-great-great-great-great-great-great- . . ."

(Is she still going?)

"great-great-great-great-granny was a *T. rex*?

What if I told you that dinosaurs AREN'T extinct?

Because birds are dinosaurs! All of us!

There are fossils that prove it!"

OK . . . but what's a fossil?

**Turn the page
and you'll see.**

FOSSILS

When a dinosaur died

near a swamp or a stream,

its body

slowly

sank.

Under sand and dirt,

the soft parts decayed,

but the skeleton stayed.

More sand, more dirt,

more mud squashed down,

so hard for so long

that the bones of the

dinosaur turned into rock.

That rock is a fossil—and a fossil is a clue.

How did this dinosaur move? What did this dinosaur do?

How long ago did this dinosaur live? What did it eat?

Without fossils, we wouldn't even know that dinosaurs existed!

FOSSIL FINDERS

Don't biff it, don't bash it,

definitely, delicately tap-tap-tap it.

Digging up a fossil can be very slow work:

you need a toothbrush, a toothpick, a chisel, a hammer,

a ruler, a pencil, a spoon, and a camera.

Then you begin ever so carefully scraping and scratching.

Drawing the bones. Weighing and measuring all of the bones.

Matching and attaching tiny little pieces to other tiny little pieces.

Like a puzzle that might take years to put together,

a skeleton starts to take shape . . .

Maybe the next incredible discovery
will show us that something in this book isn't true.
Maybe it will be found by somebody reading this book.
Somebody like YOU!

A DINOSAUR TIME LINE

A really, really, really long time ago
THE TRIASSIC PERIOD

During the Triassic, Earth was a hot, hot planet, with hardly any rain and no flowers. The first dinosaurs were small and tough, and there weren't many of them around yet. They were up against extreme weather, endless volcanic eruptions, and fierce reptiles much bigger than them. Somehow, they survived!

Triassic dinosaurs in this book:
Coelophysis, *Eoraptor*,
and *Herrerasaurus*

A really, really long time ago
THE JURASSIC PERIOD

During the Jurassic, there were massive lush green forests everywhere—and more dinosaurs than ever, all across the earth. There were giant long-necked sauropods, munching on trees. There were giant therapod predators, hunting and munching on sauropods. There were tough armored plant eaters, plodding about, and smaller scurriers, who were, well, just . . . scurrying. Dinosaurs everywhere!

Some of the Jurassic dinosaurs in this book:
Allosaurus, *Brachiosaurus*, *Diplodocus*,
and *Stegosaurus*

				TRIASSIC			JURASSIC		
300 million years ago			**250**				**200**		
			First dinosaurs						

AGE OF THE

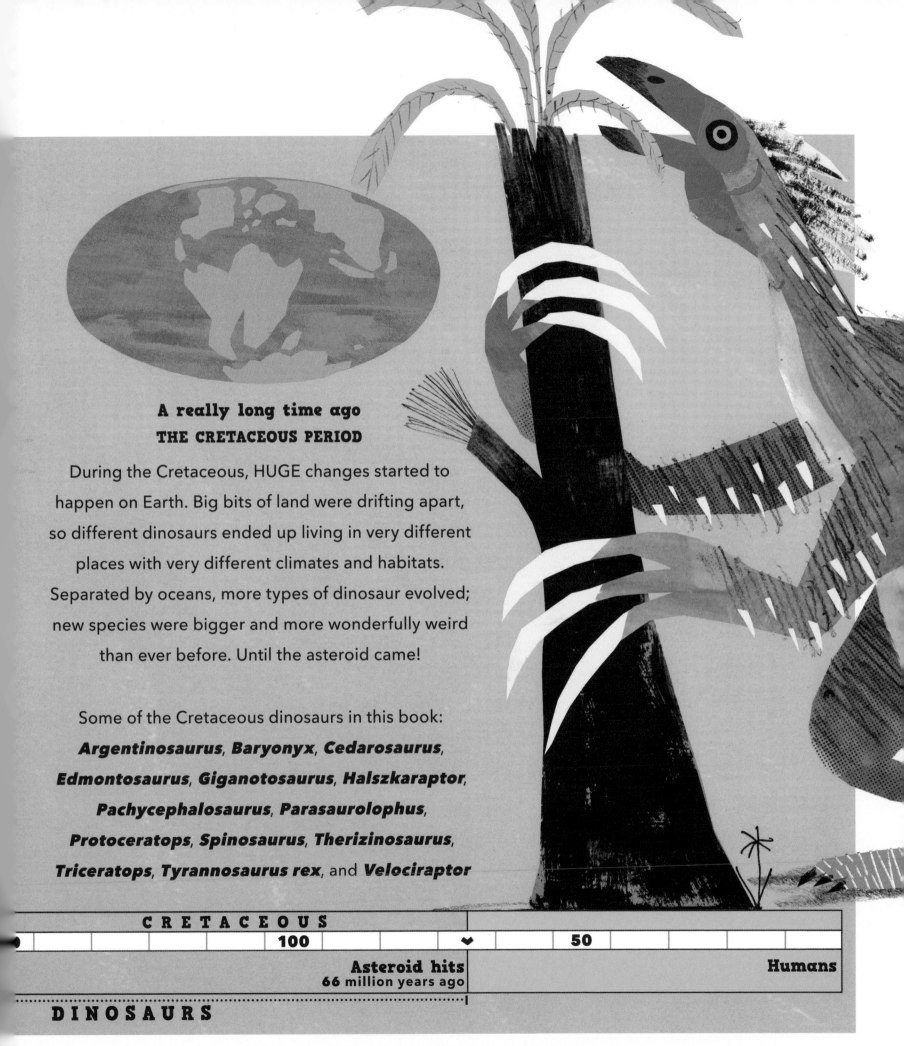

A really long time ago
THE CRETACEOUS PERIOD

During the Cretaceous, HUGE changes started to happen on Earth. Big bits of land were drifting apart, so different dinosaurs ended up living in very different places with very different climates and habitats. Separated by oceans, more types of dinosaur evolved; new species were bigger and more wonderfully weird than ever before. Until the asteroid came!

Some of the Cretaceous dinosaurs in this book:

Argentinosaurus, *Baryonyx*, *Cedarosaurus*, *Edmontosaurus*, *Giganotosaurus*, *Halszkaraptor*, *Pachycephalosaurus*, *Parasaurolophus*, *Protoceratops*, *Spinosaurus*, *Therizinosaurus*, *Triceratops*, *Tyrannosaurus rex*, and *Velociraptor*

CRETACEOUS		
100	❤	50
Asteroid hits 66 million years ago		**Humans**

DINOSAURS

For Mum, Nicki, Ivan, Frances,
and Gecko—thanks for
your listening ears and
excellent advice!
SM

For Maxwell
MH

With thanks to Dr. Nick Crumpton
for his expertise and advice

Text copyright © 2023 by Simon Mole
Illustrations copyright © 2023 by Matt Hunt

First US edition 2023
First published by Walker Books Ltd. (UK) 2023

Library of Congress Catalog Card Number 2023900231
ISBN 978-1-5362-3124-3

23 24 25 26 27 28 LEO 10 9 8 7 6 5 4 3 2 1

Printed in Heshan, Guangdong, China

This book was typeset in HVD Comic Serif and Avenir Next.
The illustrations were done in mixed media.

Candlewick Press
99 Dover Street
Somerville, Massachusetts 02144

www.candlewick.com